I0455968

A FLEXIBLE
DAY TIMER

START AT ANY TIME

JOAN MARIE VERBA

2014

January

S	M	T	W	T	F	S
			1	2	3	4
5	6	7	8	9	10	11
12	13	14	15	16	17	18
19	20	21	22	23	24	25
26	27	28	29	30	31	

February

S	M	T	W	T	F	S
						1
2	3	4	5	6	7	8
9	10	11	12	13	14	15
16	17	18	19	20	21	22
23	24	25	26	27	28	

March

S	M	T	W	T	F	S
						1
2	3	4	5	6	7	8
9	10	11	12	13	14	15
16	17	18	19	20	21	22
23	24	25	26	27	28	29
30	31					

April

S	M	T	W	T	F	S
		1	2	3	4	5
6	7	8	9	10	11	12
13	14	15	16	17	18	19
20	21	22	23	24	25	26
27	28	29	30			

May

S	M	T	W	T	F	S
				1	2	3
4	5	6	7	8	9	10
11	12	13	14	15	16	17
18	19	20	21	22	23	24
25	26	27	28	29	30	31

June

S	M	T	W	T	F	S
1	2	3	4	5	6	7
8	9	10	11	12	13	14
15	16	17	18	19	20	21
22	23	24	25	26	27	28
29	30					

July

S	M	T	W	T	F	S
		1	2	3	4	5
6	7	8	9	10	11	12
13	14	15	16	17	18	19
20	21	22	23	24	25	26
27	28	29	30	31		

August

S	M	T	W	T	F	S
					1	2
3	4	5	6	7	8	9
10	11	12	13	14	15	16
17	18	19	20	21	22	23
24	25	26	27	28	29	30
31						

September

S	M	T	W	T	F	S
	1	2	3	4	5	6
7	8	9	10	11	12	13
14	15	16	17	18	19	20
21	22	23	24	25	26	27
28	29	30				

October

S	M	T	W	T	F	S
			1	2	3	4
5	6	7	8	9	10	11
12	13	14	15	16	17	18
19	20	21	22	23	24	25
26	27	28	29	30	31	

November

S	M	T	W	T	F	S
						1
2	3	4	5	6	7	8
9	10	11	12	13	14	15
16	17	18	19	20	21	22
23	24	25	26	27	28	29
30						

December

S	M	T	W	T	F	S
	1	2	3	4	5	6
7	8	9	10	11	12	13
14	15	16	17	18	19	20
21	22	23	24	25	26	27
28	29	30	31			

2015

January

S	M	T	W	T	F	S
				1	2	3
4	5	6	7	8	9	10
11	12	13	14	15	16	17
18	19	20	21	22	23	24
25	26	27	28	29	30	31

February

S	M	T	W	T	F	S
1	2	3	4	5	6	7
8	9	10	11	12	13	14
15	16	17	18	19	20	21
22	23	24	25	26	27	28

March

S	M	T	W	T	F	S
1	2	3	4	5	6	7
8	9	10	11	12	13	14
15	16	17	18	19	20	21
22	23	24	25	26	27	28
29	30	31				

April

S	M	T	W	T	F	S
			1	2	3	4
5	6	7	8	9	10	11
12	13	14	15	16	17	18
19	20	21	22	23	24	25
26	27	28	29	30		

May

S	M	T	W	T	F	S
					1	2
3	4	5	6	7	8	9
10	11	12	13	14	15	16
17	18	19	20	21	22	23
24	25	26	27	28	29	30
31						

June

S	M	T	W	T	F	S
	1	2	3	4	5	6
7	8	9	10	11	12	13
14	15	16	17	18	19	20
21	22	23	24	25	26	27
28	29	30				

July

S	M	T	W	T	F	S
			1	2	3	4
5	6	7	8	9	10	11
12	13	14	15	16	17	18
19	20	21	22	23	24	25
26	27	28	29	30	31	

August

S	M	T	W	T	F	S
						1
2	3	4	5	6	7	8
9	10	11	12	13	14	15
16	17	18	19	20	21	22
23	24	25	26	27	28	29
30	31					

September

S	M	T	W	T	F	S
		1	2	3	4	5
6	7	8	9	10	11	12
13	14	15	16	17	18	19
20	21	22	23	24	25	26
27	28	29	30			

October

S	M	T	W	T	F	S
				1	2	3
4	5	6	7	8	9	10
11	12	13	14	15	16	17
18	19	20	21	22	23	24
25	26	27	28	29	30	31

November

S	M	T	W	T	F	S
1	2	3	4	5	6	7
8	9	10	11	12	13	14
15	16	17	18	19	20	21
22	23	24	25	26	27	28
29	30					

December

S	M	T	W	T	F	S
		1	2	3	4	5
6	7	8	9	10	11	12
13	14	15	16	17	18	19
20	21	22	23	24	25	26
27	28	29	30	31		

Date:	Date:
6 am	6 am
7 am	7 am
8 am	8 am
9 am	9 am
10 am	10 am
11am	11am
12 noon	12 noon
1 pm	1 pm
2 pm	2 pm
3 pm	3 pm
4 pm	4 pm
5 pm	5 pm
6 pm	6 pm
Notes:	Notes:

Date:	Date:
6 am	6 am
7 am	7 am
8 am	8 am
9 am	9 am
10 am	10 am
11am	11am
12 noon	12 noon
1 pm	1 pm
2 pm	2 pm
3 pm	3 pm
4 pm	4 pm
5 pm	5 pm
6 pm	6 pm
Notes:	Notes:

Date:	Date:
6 am	6 am
7 am	7 am
8 am	8 am
9 am	9 am
10 am	10 am
11am	11am
12 noon	12 noon
1 pm	1 pm
2 pm	2 pm
3 pm	3 pm
4 pm	4 pm
5 pm	5 pm
6 pm	6 pm
Notes:	Notes:

Date:	Date:
6 am	6 am
7 am	7 am
8 am	8 am
9 am	9 am
10 am	10 am
11am	11am
12 noon	12 noon
1 pm	1 pm
2 pm	2 pm
3 pm	3 pm
4 pm	4 pm
5 pm	5 pm
6 pm	6 pm
Notes:	Notes:

Date:	Date:
6 am	6 am
7 am	7 am
8 am	8 am
9 am	9 am
10 am	10 am
11am	11am
12 noon	12 noon
1 pm	1 pm
2 pm	2 pm
3 pm	3 pm
4 pm	4 pm
5 pm	5 pm
6 pm	6 pm
Notes:	Notes:

Date: _____ | Date: _____

6 am	6 am
7 am	7 am
8 am	8 am
9 am	9 am
10 am	10 am
11am	11am
12 noon	12 noon
1 pm	1 pm
2 pm	2 pm
3 pm	3 pm
4 pm	4 pm
5 pm	5 pm
6 pm	6 pm
Notes:	Notes:

Date:	Date:
6 am	6 am
7 am	7 am
8 am	8 am
9 am	9 am
10 am	10 am
11am	11am
12 noon	12 noon
1 pm	1 pm
2 pm	2 pm
3 pm	3 pm
4 pm	4 pm
5 pm	5 pm
6 pm	6 pm
Notes:	Notes:

Date: _____   Date: _____

6 am	6 am
7 am	7 am
8 am	8 am
9 am	9 am
10 am	10 am
11am	11am
12 noon	12 noon
1 pm	1 pm
2 pm	2 pm
3 pm	3 pm
4 pm	4 pm
5 pm	5 pm
6 pm	6 pm
Notes:	Notes:

Date:	Date:
6 am	6 am
7 am	7 am
8 am	8 am
9 am	9 am
10 am	10 am
11am	11am
12 noon	12 noon
1 pm	1 pm
2 pm	2 pm
3 pm	3 pm
4 pm	4 pm
5 pm	5 pm
6 pm	6 pm
Notes:	Notes:

Date:	Date:
6 am	6 am
7 am	7 am
8 am	8 am
9 am	9 am
10 am	10 am
11am	11am
12 noon	12 noon
1 pm	1 pm
2 pm	2 pm
3 pm	3 pm
4 pm	4 pm
5 pm	5 pm
6 pm	6 pm
Notes:	Notes:

Date:	Date:
6 am	6 am
7 am	7 am
8 am	8 am
9 am	9 am
10 am	10 am
11am	11am
12 noon	12 noon
1 pm	1 pm
2 pm	2 pm
3 pm	3 pm
4 pm	4 pm
5 pm	5 pm
6 pm	6 pm
Notes:	Notes:

Date:	Date:
6 am	6 am
7 am	7 am
8 am	8 am
9 am	9 am
10 am	10 am
11am	11am
12 noon	12 noon
1 pm	1 pm
2 pm	2 pm
3 pm	3 pm
4 pm	4 pm
5 pm	5 pm
6 pm	6 pm
Notes:	Notes:

Date:	Date:
6 am	6 am
7 am	7 am
8 am	8 am
9 am	9 am
10 am	10 am
11am	11am
12 noon	12 noon
1 pm	1 pm
2 pm	2 pm
3 pm	3 pm
4 pm	4 pm
5 pm	5 pm
6 pm	6 pm
Notes:	Notes:

Date:	Date:
6 am	6 am
7 am	7 am
8 am	8 am
9 am	9 am
10 am	10 am
11am	11am
12 noon	12 noon
1 pm	1 pm
2 pm	2 pm
3 pm	3 pm
4 pm	4 pm
5 pm	5 pm
6 pm	6 pm
Notes:	Notes:

Date: _____

6 am	
7 am	
8 am	
9 am	
10 am	
11am	
12 noon	
1 pm	
2 pm	
3 pm	
4 pm	
5 pm	
6 pm	
Notes:	

Date: _____

6 am	
7 am	
8 am	
9 am	
10 am	
11am	
12 noon	
1 pm	
2 pm	
3 pm	
4 pm	
5 pm	
6 pm	
Notes:	

Date: _____

6 am	6 am
7 am	7 am
8 am	8 am
9 am	9 am
10 am	10 am
11am	11am
12 noon	12 noon
1 pm	1 pm
2 pm	2 pm
3 pm	3 pm
4 pm	4 pm
5 pm	5 pm
6 pm	6 pm
Notes:	Notes:

Date:	Date:
6 am	6 am
7 am	7 am
8 am	8 am
9 am	9 am
10 am	10 am
11am	11am
12 noon	12 noon
1 pm	1 pm
2 pm	2 pm
3 pm	3 pm
4 pm	4 pm
5 pm	5 pm
6 pm	6 pm
Notes:	Notes:

Date:	Date:
6 am	6 am
7 am	7 am
8 am	8 am
9 am	9 am
10 am	10 am
11am	11am
12 noon	12 noon
1 pm	1 pm
2 pm	2 pm
3 pm	3 pm
4 pm	4 pm
5 pm	5 pm
6 pm	6 pm
Notes:	Notes:

Date:	Date:
6 am	6 am
7 am	7 am
8 am	8 am
9 am	9 am
10 am	10 am
11am	11am
12 noon	12 noon
1 pm	1 pm
2 pm	2 pm
3 pm	3 pm
4 pm	4 pm
5 pm	5 pm
6 pm	6 pm
Notes:	Notes:

Date:	Date:
6 am	6 am
7 am	7 am
8 am	8 am
9 am	9 am
10 am	10 am
11am	11am
12 noon	12 noon
1 pm	1 pm
2 pm	2 pm
3 pm	3 pm
4 pm	4 pm
5 pm	5 pm
6 pm	6 pm
Notes:	Notes:

Date:	Date:
6 am	6 am
7 am	7 am
8 am	8 am
9 am	9 am
10 am	10 am
11am	11am
12 noon	12 noon
1 pm	1 pm
2 pm	2 pm
3 pm	3 pm
4 pm	4 pm
5 pm	5 pm
6 pm	6 pm
Notes:	Notes:

Date:	Date:
6 am	6 am
7 am	7 am
8 am	8 am
9 am	9 am
10 am	10 am
11am	11am
12 noon	12 noon
1 pm	1 pm
2 pm	2 pm
3 pm	3 pm
4 pm	4 pm
5 pm	5 pm
6 pm	6 pm
Notes:	Notes:

Date:	Date:
6 am	6 am
7 am	7 am
8 am	8 am
9 am	9 am
10 am	10 am
11am	11am
12 noon	12 noon
1 pm	1 pm
2 pm	2 pm
3 pm	3 pm
4 pm	4 pm
5 pm	5 pm
6 pm	6 pm
Notes:	Notes:

Date:	Date:
6 am	6 am
7 am	7 am
8 am	8 am
9 am	9 am
10 am	10 am
11am	11am
12 noon	12 noon
1 pm	1 pm
2 pm	2 pm
3 pm	3 pm
4 pm	4 pm
5 pm	5 pm
6 pm	6 pm
Notes:	Notes:

Date:	Date:
6 am	6 am
7 am	7 am
8 am	8 am
9 am	9 am
10 am	10 am
11am	11am
12 noon	12 noon
1 pm	1 pm
2 pm	2 pm
3 pm	3 pm
4 pm	4 pm
5 pm	5 pm
6 pm	6 pm
Notes:	Notes:

Date:	Date:
6 am	6 am
7 am	7 am
8 am	8 am
9 am	9 am
10 am	10 am
11am	11am
12 noon	12 noon
1 pm	1 pm
2 pm	2 pm
3 pm	3 pm
4 pm	4 pm
5 pm	5 pm
6 pm	6 pm
Notes:	Notes:

Date:	Date:
6 am	6 am
7 am	7 am
8 am	8 am
9 am	9 am
10 am	10 am
11am	11am
12 noon	12 noon
1 pm	1 pm
2 pm	2 pm
3 pm	3 pm
4 pm	4 pm
5 pm	5 pm
6 pm	6 pm
Notes:	Notes:

Date:	Date:
6 am	6 am
7 am	7 am
8 am	8 am
9 am	9 am
10 am	10 am
11am	11am
12 noon	12 noon
1 pm	1 pm
2 pm	2 pm
3 pm	3 pm
4 pm	4 pm
5 pm	5 pm
6 pm	6 pm
Notes:	Notes:

Date:	Date:
6 am	6 am
7 am	7 am
8 am	8 am
9 am	9 am
10 am	10 am
11am	11am
12 noon	12 noon
1 pm	1 pm
2 pm	2 pm
3 pm	3 pm
4 pm	4 pm
5 pm	5 pm
6 pm	6 pm
Notes:	Notes:

Date: | Date:

6 am	6 am
7 am	7 am
8 am	8 am
9 am	9 am
10 am	10 am
11am	11am
12 noon	12 noon
1 pm	1 pm
2 pm	2 pm
3 pm	3 pm
4 pm	4 pm
5 pm	5 pm
6 pm	6 pm
Notes:	Notes:

Date:	Date:
6 am	6 am
7 am	7 am
8 am	8 am
9 am	9 am
10 am	10 am
11am	11am
12 noon	12 noon
1 pm	1 pm
2 pm	2 pm
3 pm	3 pm
4 pm	4 pm
5 pm	5 pm
6 pm	6 pm
Notes:	Notes:

Date:	Date:
6 am	6 am
7 am	7 am
8 am	8 am
9 am	9 am
10 am	10 am
11am	11am
12 noon	12 noon
1 pm	1 pm
2 pm	2 pm
3 pm	3 pm
4 pm	4 pm
5 pm	5 pm
6 pm	6 pm
Notes:	Notes:

Date:	Date:
6 am	6 am
7 am	7 am
8 am	8 am
9 am	9 am
10 am	10 am
11am	11am
12 noon	12 noon
1 pm	1 pm
2 pm	2 pm
3 pm	3 pm
4 pm	4 pm
5 pm	5 pm
6 pm	6 pm
Notes:	Notes:

Date:	Date:
6 am	6 am
7 am	7 am
8 am	8 am
9 am	9 am
10 am	10 am
11am	11am
12 noon	12 noon
1 pm	1 pm
2 pm	2 pm
3 pm	3 pm
4 pm	4 pm
5 pm	5 pm
6 pm	6 pm
Notes:	Notes:

Date:	Date:
6 am	6 am
7 am	7 am
8 am	8 am
9 am	9 am
10 am	10 am
11am	11am
12 noon	12 noon
1 pm	1 pm
2 pm	2 pm
3 pm	3 pm
4 pm	4 pm
5 pm	5 pm
6 pm	6 pm
Notes:	Notes:

Date:	Date:
6 am	6 am
7 am	7 am
8 am	8 am
9 am	9 am
10 am	10 am
11am	11am
12 noon	12 noon
1 pm	1 pm
2 pm	2 pm
3 pm	3 pm
4 pm	4 pm
5 pm	5 pm
6 pm	6 pm
Notes:	Notes:

Date:	Date:
6 am	6 am
7 am	7 am
8 am	8 am
9 am	9 am
10 am	10 am
11am	11am
12 noon	12 noon
1 pm	1 pm
2 pm	2 pm
3 pm	3 pm
4 pm	4 pm
5 pm	5 pm
6 pm	6 pm
Notes:	Notes:

Date:	Date:
6 am	6 am
7 am	7 am
8 am	8 am
9 am	9 am
10 am	10 am
11am	11am
12 noon	12 noon
1 pm	1 pm
2 pm	2 pm
3 pm	3 pm
4 pm	4 pm
5 pm	5 pm
6 pm	6 pm
Notes:	Notes:

Date:	Date:
6 am	6 am
7 am	7 am
8 am	8 am
9 am	9 am
10 am	10 am
11am	11am
12 noon	12 noon
1 pm	1 pm
2 pm	2 pm
3 pm	3 pm
4 pm	4 pm
5 pm	5 pm
6 pm	6 pm
Notes:	Notes:

Date:	Date:
6 am	6 am
7 am	7 am
8 am	8 am
9 am	9 am
10 am	10 am
11am	11am
12 noon	12 noon
1 pm	1 pm
2 pm	2 pm
3 pm	3 pm
4 pm	4 pm
5 pm	5 pm
6 pm	6 pm
Notes:	Notes:

Date:	Date:
6 am	6 am
7 am	7 am
8 am	8 am
9 am	9 am
10 am	10 am
11am	11am
12 noon	12 noon
1 pm	1 pm
2 pm	2 pm
3 pm	3 pm
4 pm	4 pm
5 pm	5 pm
6 pm	6 pm
Notes:	Notes:

Date:	Date:
6 am	6 am
7 am	7 am
8 am	8 am
9 am	9 am
10 am	10 am
11am	11am
12 noon	12 noon
1 pm	1 pm
2 pm	2 pm
3 pm	3 pm
4 pm	4 pm
5 pm	5 pm
6 pm	6 pm
Notes:	Notes:

Date:	Date:
6 am	6 am
7 am	7 am
8 am	8 am
9 am	9 am
10 am	10 am
11am	11am
12 noon	12 noon
1 pm	1 pm
2 pm	2 pm
3 pm	3 pm
4 pm	4 pm
5 pm	5 pm
6 pm	6 pm
Notes:	Notes:

Date:	Date:
6 am	6 am
7 am	7 am
8 am	8 am
9 am	9 am
10 am	10 am
11am	11am
12 noon	12 noon
1 pm	1 pm
2 pm	2 pm
3 pm	3 pm
4 pm	4 pm
5 pm	5 pm
6 pm	6 pm
Notes:	Notes:

Date:	Date:
6 am	6 am
7 am	7 am
8 am	8 am
9 am	9 am
10 am	10 am
11am	11am
12 noon	12 noon
1 pm	1 pm
2 pm	2 pm
3 pm	3 pm
4 pm	4 pm
5 pm	5 pm
6 pm	6 pm
Notes:	Notes:

Date:	Date:
6 am	6 am
7 am	7 am
8 am	8 am
9 am	9 am
10 am	10 am
11am	11am
12 noon	12 noon
1 pm	1 pm
2 pm	2 pm
3 pm	3 pm
4 pm	4 pm
5 pm	5 pm
6 pm	6 pm
Notes:	Notes:

Date:	Date:
6 am	6 am
7 am	7 am
8 am	8 am
9 am	9 am
10 am	10 am
11am	11am
12 noon	12 noon
1 pm	1 pm
2 pm	2 pm
3 pm	3 pm
4 pm	4 pm
5 pm	5 pm
6 pm	6 pm
Notes:	Notes:

Date:	Date:
6 am	6 am
7 am	7 am
8 am	8 am
9 am	9 am
10 am	10 am
11am	11am
12 noon	12 noon
1 pm	1 pm
2 pm	2 pm
3 pm	3 pm
4 pm	4 pm
5 pm	5 pm
6 pm	6 pm
Notes:	Notes:

Date: | Date:

6 am	6 am
7 am	7 am
8 am	8 am
9 am	9 am
10 am	10 am
11am	11am
12 noon	12 noon
1 pm	1 pm
2 pm	2 pm
3 pm	3 pm
4 pm	4 pm
5 pm	5 pm
6 pm	6 pm
Notes:	Notes:

Date:	Date:
6 am	6 am
7 am	7 am
8 am	8 am
9 am	9 am
10 am	10 am
11am	11am
12 noon	12 noon
1 pm	1 pm
2 pm	2 pm
3 pm	3 pm
4 pm	4 pm
5 pm	5 pm
6 pm	6 pm
Notes:	Notes:

Date:	Date:
6 am	6 am
7 am	7 am
8 am	8 am
9 am	9 am
10 am	10 am
11am	11am
12 noon	12 noon
1 pm	1 pm
2 pm	2 pm
3 pm	3 pm
4 pm	4 pm
5 pm	5 pm
6 pm	6 pm
Notes:	Notes:

Date:	Date:
6 am	6 am
7 am	7 am
8 am	8 am
9 am	9 am
10 am	10 am
11am	11am
12 noon	12 noon
1 pm	1 pm
2 pm	2 pm
3 pm	3 pm
4 pm	4 pm
5 pm	5 pm
6 pm	6 pm
Notes:	Notes:

Date:	Date:
6 am	6 am
7 am	7 am
8 am	8 am
9 am	9 am
10 am	10 am
11am	11am
12 noon	12 noon
1 pm	1 pm
2 pm	2 pm
3 pm	3 pm
4 pm	4 pm
5 pm	5 pm
6 pm	6 pm
Notes:	Notes:

Date: | Date:

6 am	6 am
7 am	7 am
8 am	8 am
9 am	9 am
10 am	10 am
11am	11am
12 noon	12 noon
1 pm	1 pm
2 pm	2 pm
3 pm	3 pm
4 pm	4 pm
5 pm	5 pm
6 pm	6 pm
Notes:	Notes:

Date: Date:

6 am	6 am
7 am	7 am
8 am	8 am
9 am	9 am
10 am	10 am
11am	11am
12 noon	12 noon
1 pm	1 pm
2 pm	2 pm
3 pm	3 pm
4 pm	4 pm
5 pm	5 pm
6 pm	6 pm
Notes:	Notes:

Date:	Date:
6 am	6 am
7 am	7 am
8 am	8 am
9 am	9 am
10 am	10 am
11am	11am
12 noon	12 noon
1 pm	1 pm
2 pm	2 pm
3 pm	3 pm
4 pm	4 pm
5 pm	5 pm
6 pm	6 pm
Notes:	Notes:

Date:	Date:
6 am	6 am
7 am	7 am
8 am	8 am
9 am	9 am
10 am	10 am
11am	11am
12 noon	12 noon
1 pm	1 pm
2 pm	2 pm
3 pm	3 pm
4 pm	4 pm
5 pm	5 pm
6 pm	6 pm
Notes:	Notes:

Date:	Date:
6 am	6 am
7 am	7 am
8 am	8 am
9 am	9 am
10 am	10 am
11am	11am
12 noon	12 noon
1 pm	1 pm
2 pm	2 pm
3 pm	3 pm
4 pm	4 pm
5 pm	5 pm
6 pm	6 pm
Notes:	Notes:

Date:	Date:
6 am	6 am
7 am	7 am
8 am	8 am
9 am	9 am
10 am	10 am
11am	11am
12 noon	12 noon
1 pm	1 pm
2 pm	2 pm
3 pm	3 pm
4 pm	4 pm
5 pm	5 pm
6 pm	6 pm
Notes:	Notes:

Date: Date:

6 am	6 am
7 am	7 am
8 am	8 am
9 am	9 am
10 am	10 am
11am	11am
12 noon	12 noon
1 pm	1 pm
2 pm	2 pm
3 pm	3 pm
4 pm	4 pm
5 pm	5 pm
6 pm	6 pm
Notes:	Notes:

Date:	Date:
6 am	6 am
7 am	7 am
8 am	8 am
9 am	9 am
10 am	10 am
11am	11am
12 noon	12 noon
1 pm	1 pm
2 pm	2 pm
3 pm	3 pm
4 pm	4 pm
5 pm	5 pm
6 pm	6 pm
Notes:	Notes:

Date:	Date:
6 am	6 am
7 am	7 am
8 am	8 am
9 am	9 am
10 am	10 am
11am	11am
12 noon	12 noon
1 pm	1 pm
2 pm	2 pm
3 pm	3 pm
4 pm	4 pm
5 pm	5 pm
6 pm	6 pm
Notes:	Notes:

Date:	Date:
6 am	6 am
7 am	7 am
8 am	8 am
9 am	9 am
10 am	10 am
11am	11am
12 noon	12 noon
1 pm	1 pm
2 pm	2 pm
3 pm	3 pm
4 pm	4 pm
5 pm	5 pm
6 pm	6 pm
Notes:	Notes:

Date:	Date:
6 am	6 am
7 am	7 am
8 am	8 am
9 am	9 am
10 am	10 am
11am	11am
12 noon	12 noon
1 pm	1 pm
2 pm	2 pm
3 pm	3 pm
4 pm	4 pm
5 pm	5 pm
6 pm	6 pm
Notes:	Notes:

Date: _____

6 am	
7 am	
8 am	
9 am	
10 am	
11am	
12 noon	
1 pm	
2 pm	
3 pm	
4 pm	
5 pm	
6 pm	

Notes:

Date: _____

6 am	
7 am	
8 am	
9 am	
10 am	
11am	
12 noon	
1 pm	
2 pm	
3 pm	
4 pm	
5 pm	
6 pm	

Notes:

Date:	Date:
6 am	6 am
7 am	7 am
8 am	8 am
9 am	9 am
10 am	10 am
11am	11am
12 noon	12 noon
1 pm	1 pm
2 pm	2 pm
3 pm	3 pm
4 pm	4 pm
5 pm	5 pm
6 pm	6 pm
Notes:	Notes:

Date:	Date:
6 am	6 am
7 am	7 am
8 am	8 am
9 am	9 am
10 am	10 am
11am	11am
12 noon	12 noon
1 pm	1 pm
2 pm	2 pm
3 pm	3 pm
4 pm	4 pm
5 pm	5 pm
6 pm	6 pm
Notes:	Notes:

Date: Date:

6 am	6 am
7 am	7 am
8 am	8 am
9 am	9 am
10 am	10 am
11am	11am
12 noon	12 noon
1 pm	1 pm
2 pm	2 pm
3 pm	3 pm
4 pm	4 pm
5 pm	5 pm
6 pm	6 pm
Notes:	Notes:

Date:	Date:
6 am	6 am
7 am	7 am
8 am	8 am
9 am	9 am
10 am	10 am
11am	11am
12 noon	12 noon
1 pm	1 pm
2 pm	2 pm
3 pm	3 pm
4 pm	4 pm
5 pm	5 pm
6 pm	6 pm
Notes:	Notes:

Date:	Date:
6 am	6 am
7 am	7 am
8 am	8 am
9 am	9 am
10 am	10 am
11am	11am
12 noon	12 noon
1 pm	1 pm
2 pm	2 pm
3 pm	3 pm
4 pm	4 pm
5 pm	5 pm
6 pm	6 pm
Notes:	Notes:

Date:	Date:
6 am	6 am
7 am	7 am
8 am	8 am
9 am	9 am
10 am	10 am
11am	11am
12 noon	12 noon
1 pm	1 pm
2 pm	2 pm
3 pm	3 pm
4 pm	4 pm
5 pm	5 pm
6 pm	6 pm
Notes:	Notes:

Date:	Date:
6 am	6 am
7 am	7 am
8 am	8 am
9 am	9 am
10 am	10 am
11am	11am
12 noon	12 noon
1 pm	1 pm
2 pm	2 pm
3 pm	3 pm
4 pm	4 pm
5 pm	5 pm
6 pm	6 pm
Notes:	Notes:

Date:	Date:
6 am	6 am
7 am	7 am
8 am	8 am
9 am	9 am
10 am	10 am
11am	11am
12 noon	12 noon
1 pm	1 pm
2 pm	2 pm
3 pm	3 pm
4 pm	4 pm
5 pm	5 pm
6 pm	6 pm
Notes:	Notes:

Date:

6 am	
7 am	
8 am	
9 am	
10 am	
11am	
12 noon	
1 pm	
2 pm	
3 pm	
4 pm	
5 pm	
6 pm	
Notes:	

Date:

6 am	
7 am	
8 am	
9 am	
10 am	
11am	
12 noon	
1 pm	
2 pm	
3 pm	
4 pm	
5 pm	
6 pm	
Notes:	

Date:	Date:
6 am	6 am
7 am	7 am
8 am	8 am
9 am	9 am
10 am	10 am
11am	11am
12 noon	12 noon
1 pm	1 pm
2 pm	2 pm
3 pm	3 pm
4 pm	4 pm
5 pm	5 pm
6 pm	6 pm
Notes:	Notes:

Date:	Date:
6 am	6 am
7 am	7 am
8 am	8 am
9 am	9 am
10 am	10 am
11am	11am
12 noon	12 noon
1 pm	1 pm
2 pm	2 pm
3 pm	3 pm
4 pm	4 pm
5 pm	5 pm
6 pm	6 pm
Notes:	Notes:

Date:	Date:
6 am	6 am
7 am	7 am
8 am	8 am
9 am	9 am
10 am	10 am
11am	11am
12 noon	12 noon
1 pm	1 pm
2 pm	2 pm
3 pm	3 pm
4 pm	4 pm
5 pm	5 pm
6 pm	6 pm
Notes:	Notes:

Date:	Date:
6 am	6 am
7 am	7 am
8 am	8 am
9 am	9 am
10 am	10 am
11am	11am
12 noon	12 noon
1 pm	1 pm
2 pm	2 pm
3 pm	3 pm
4 pm	4 pm
5 pm	5 pm
6 pm	6 pm
Notes:	Notes:

Date:	Date:
6 am	6 am
7 am	7 am
8 am	8 am
9 am	9 am
10 am	10 am
11am	11am
12 noon	12 noon
1 pm	1 pm
2 pm	2 pm
3 pm	3 pm
4 pm	4 pm
5 pm	5 pm
6 pm	6 pm
Notes:	Notes:

Date:

6 am
7 am
8 am
9 am
10 am
11am
12 noon
1 pm
2 pm
3 pm
4 pm
5 pm
6 pm
Notes:

Date:

6 am
7 am
8 am
9 am
10 am
11am
12 noon
1 pm
2 pm
3 pm
4 pm
5 pm
6 pm
Notes:

Date:	Date:
6 am	6 am
7 am	7 am
8 am	8 am
9 am	9 am
10 am	10 am
11am	11am
12 noon	12 noon
1 pm	1 pm
2 pm	2 pm
3 pm	3 pm
4 pm	4 pm
5 pm	5 pm
6 pm	6 pm
Notes:	Notes:

Date:	Date:
6 am	6 am
7 am	7 am
8 am	8 am
9 am	9 am
10 am	10 am
11am	11am
12 noon	12 noon
1 pm	1 pm
2 pm	2 pm
3 pm	3 pm
4 pm	4 pm
5 pm	5 pm
6 pm	6 pm
Notes:	Notes:

Date:	Date:
6 am	6 am
7 am	7 am
8 am	8 am
9 am	9 am
10 am	10 am
11am	11am
12 noon	12 noon
1 pm	1 pm
2 pm	2 pm
3 pm	3 pm
4 pm	4 pm
5 pm	5 pm
6 pm	6 pm
Notes:	Notes:

Date:	Date:
6 am	6 am
7 am	7 am
8 am	8 am
9 am	9 am
10 am	10 am
11am	11am
12 noon	12 noon
1 pm	1 pm
2 pm	2 pm
3 pm	3 pm
4 pm	4 pm
5 pm	5 pm
6 pm	6 pm
Notes:	Notes:

Date:	Date:
6 am	6 am
7 am	7 am
8 am	8 am
9 am	9 am
10 am	10 am
11am	11am
12 noon	12 noon
1 pm	1 pm
2 pm	2 pm
3 pm	3 pm
4 pm	4 pm
5 pm	5 pm
6 pm	6 pm
Notes:	Notes:

Date:	Date:
6 am	6 am
7 am	7 am
8 am	8 am
9 am	9 am
10 am	10 am
11am	11am
12 noon	12 noon
1 pm	1 pm
2 pm	2 pm
3 pm	3 pm
4 pm	4 pm
5 pm	5 pm
6 pm	6 pm
Notes:	Notes:

Date:	Date:
6 am	6 am
7 am	7 am
8 am	8 am
9 am	9 am
10 am	10 am
11am	11am
12 noon	12 noon
1 pm	1 pm
2 pm	2 pm
3 pm	3 pm
4 pm	4 pm
5 pm	5 pm
6 pm	6 pm
Notes:	Notes:

Date:	Date:
6 am	6 am
7 am	7 am
8 am	8 am
9 am	9 am
10 am	10 am
11am	11am
12 noon	12 noon
1 pm	1 pm
2 pm	2 pm
3 pm	3 pm
4 pm	4 pm
5 pm	5 pm
6 pm	6 pm
Notes:	Notes:

Date:	Date:
6 am	6 am
7 am	7 am
8 am	8 am
9 am	9 am
10 am	10 am
11am	11am
12 noon	12 noon
1 pm	1 pm
2 pm	2 pm
3 pm	3 pm
4 pm	4 pm
5 pm	5 pm
6 pm	6 pm
Notes:	Notes:

Date:	Date:
6 am	6 am
7 am	7 am
8 am	8 am
9 am	9 am
10 am	10 am
11am	11am
12 noon	12 noon
1 pm	1 pm
2 pm	2 pm
3 pm	3 pm
4 pm	4 pm
5 pm	5 pm
6 pm	6 pm
Notes:	Notes:

Date:	Date:
6 am	6 am
7 am	7 am
8 am	8 am
9 am	9 am
10 am	10 am
11am	11am
12 noon	12 noon
1 pm	1 pm
2 pm	2 pm
3 pm	3 pm
4 pm	4 pm
5 pm	5 pm
6 pm	6 pm
Notes:	Notes:

Date:	Date:
6 am	6 am
7 am	7 am
8 am	8 am
9 am	9 am
10 am	10 am
11am	11am
12 noon	12 noon
1 pm	1 pm
2 pm	2 pm
3 pm	3 pm
4 pm	4 pm
5 pm	5 pm
6 pm	6 pm
Notes:	Notes:

Date:	Date:
6 am	6 am
7 am	7 am
8 am	8 am
9 am	9 am
10 am	10 am
11am	11am
12 noon	12 noon
1 pm	1 pm
2 pm	2 pm
3 pm	3 pm
4 pm	4 pm
5 pm	5 pm
6 pm	6 pm
Notes:	Notes:

Date:	Date:
6 am	6 am
7 am	7 am
8 am	8 am
9 am	9 am
10 am	10 am
11am	11am
12 noon	12 noon
1 pm	1 pm
2 pm	2 pm
3 pm	3 pm
4 pm	4 pm
5 pm	5 pm
6 pm	6 pm
Notes:	Notes:

Date:	Date:
6 am	6 am
7 am	7 am
8 am	8 am
9 am	9 am
10 am	10 am
11am	11am
12 noon	12 noon
1 pm	1 pm
2 pm	2 pm
3 pm	3 pm
4 pm	4 pm
5 pm	5 pm
6 pm	6 pm
Notes:	Notes:

Date:	Date:
6 am	6 am
7 am	7 am
8 am	8 am
9 am	9 am
10 am	10 am
11am	11am
12 noon	12 noon
1 pm	1 pm
2 pm	2 pm
3 pm	3 pm
4 pm	4 pm
5 pm	5 pm
6 pm	6 pm
Notes:	Notes:

Date:	Date:
6 am	6 am
7 am	7 am
8 am	8 am
9 am	9 am
10 am	10 am
11am	11am
12 noon	12 noon
1 pm	1 pm
2 pm	2 pm
3 pm	3 pm
4 pm	4 pm
5 pm	5 pm
6 pm	6 pm
Notes:	Notes:

Date:	Date:
6 am	6 am
7 am	7 am
8 am	8 am
9 am	9 am
10 am	10 am
11am	11am
12 noon	12 noon
1 pm	1 pm
2 pm	2 pm
3 pm	3 pm
4 pm	4 pm
5 pm	5 pm
6 pm	6 pm
Notes:	Notes:

Date:	Date:
6 am	6 am
7 am	7 am
8 am	8 am
9 am	9 am
10 am	10 am
11am	11am
12 noon	12 noon
1 pm	1 pm
2 pm	2 pm
3 pm	3 pm
4 pm	4 pm
5 pm	5 pm
6 pm	6 pm
Notes:	Notes:

Date:	Date:
6 am	6 am
7 am	7 am
8 am	8 am
9 am	9 am
10 am	10 am
11am	11am
12 noon	12 noon
1 pm	1 pm
2 pm	2 pm
3 pm	3 pm
4 pm	4 pm
5 pm	5 pm
6 pm	6 pm
Notes:	Notes:

Date:	Date:
6 am	6 am
7 am	7 am
8 am	8 am
9 am	9 am
10 am	10 am
11am	11am
12 noon	12 noon
1 pm	1 pm
2 pm	2 pm
3 pm	3 pm
4 pm	4 pm
5 pm	5 pm
6 pm	6 pm
Notes:	Notes:

Date:	Date:
6 am	6 am
7 am	7 am
8 am	8 am
9 am	9 am
10 am	10 am
11am	11am
12 noon	12 noon
1 pm	1 pm
2 pm	2 pm
3 pm	3 pm
4 pm	4 pm
5 pm	5 pm
6 pm	6 pm
Notes:	Notes:

Date:	Date:
6 am	6 am
7 am	7 am
8 am	8 am
9 am	9 am
10 am	10 am
11am	11am
12 noon	12 noon
1 pm	1 pm
2 pm	2 pm
3 pm	3 pm
4 pm	4 pm
5 pm	5 pm
6 pm	6 pm
Notes:	Notes:

Date:	Date:
6 am	6 am
7 am	7 am
8 am	8 am
9 am	9 am
10 am	10 am
11am	11am
12 noon	12 noon
1 pm	1 pm
2 pm	2 pm
3 pm	3 pm
4 pm	4 pm
5 pm	5 pm
6 pm	6 pm
Notes:	Notes:

Date:	Date:
6 am	6 am
7 am	7 am
8 am	8 am
9 am	9 am
10 am	10 am
11am	11am
12 noon	12 noon
1 pm	1 pm
2 pm	2 pm
3 pm	3 pm
4 pm	4 pm
5 pm	5 pm
6 pm	6 pm
Notes:	Notes:

Date:	Date:
6 am	6 am
7 am	7 am
8 am	8 am
9 am	9 am
10 am	10 am
11am	11am
12 noon	12 noon
1 pm	1 pm
2 pm	2 pm
3 pm	3 pm
4 pm	4 pm
5 pm	5 pm
6 pm	6 pm
Notes:	Notes:

Date: _____

| Date: _____ |

| 6 am |
| |
| 7 am |
| |
| 8 am |
| |
| 9 am |
| |
| 10 am |
| |
| 11am |
| |
| 12 noon |
| |
| 1 pm |
| |
| 2 pm |
| |
| 3 pm |
| |
| 4 pm |
| |
| 5 pm |
| |
| 6 pm |
| |
| Notes: |
| |
| |
| |
| |
| |
| |

Date: _____

| 6 am |
| |
| 7 am |
| |
| 8 am |
| |
| 9 am |
| |
| 10 am |
| |
| 11am |
| |
| 12 noon |
| |
| 1 pm |
| |
| 2 pm |
| |
| 3 pm |
| |
| 4 pm |
| |
| 5 pm |
| |
| 6 pm |
| |
| Notes: |
| |
| |
| |
| |
| |
| |

Date:	Date:
6 am	6 am
7 am	7 am
8 am	8 am
9 am	9 am
10 am	10 am
11am	11am
12 noon	12 noon
1 pm	1 pm
2 pm	2 pm
3 pm	3 pm
4 pm	4 pm
5 pm	5 pm
6 pm	6 pm
Notes:	Notes:

Date: _____

6 am	
7 am	
8 am	
9 am	
10 am	
11am	
12 noon	
1 pm	
2 pm	
3 pm	
4 pm	
5 pm	
6 pm	
Notes:	

Date: _____

6 am	
7 am	
8 am	
9 am	
10 am	
11am	
12 noon	
1 pm	
2 pm	
3 pm	
4 pm	
5 pm	
6 pm	
Notes:	

Date:	Date:
6 am	6 am
7 am	7 am
8 am	8 am
9 am	9 am
10 am	10 am
11am	11am
12 noon	12 noon
1 pm	1 pm
2 pm	2 pm
3 pm	3 pm
4 pm	4 pm
5 pm	5 pm
6 pm	6 pm
Notes:	Notes:

Date:	Date:
6 am	6 am
7 am	7 am
8 am	8 am
9 am	9 am
10 am	10 am
11am	11am
12 noon	12 noon
1 pm	1 pm
2 pm	2 pm
3 pm	3 pm
4 pm	4 pm
5 pm	5 pm
6 pm	6 pm
Notes:	Notes:

Date: | Date:

6 am	6 am
7 am	7 am
8 am	8 am
9 am	9 am
10 am	10 am
11am	11am
12 noon	12 noon
1 pm	1 pm
2 pm	2 pm
3 pm	3 pm
4 pm	4 pm
5 pm	5 pm
6 pm	6 pm
Notes:	Notes:

Date:	Date:
6 am	6 am
7 am	7 am
8 am	8 am
9 am	9 am
10 am	10 am
11am	11am
12 noon	12 noon
1 pm	1 pm
2 pm	2 pm
3 pm	3 pm
4 pm	4 pm
5 pm	5 pm
6 pm	6 pm
Notes:	Notes:

Date:	Date:
6 am	6 am
7 am	7 am
8 am	8 am
9 am	9 am
10 am	10 am
11am	11am
12 noon	12 noon
1 pm	1 pm
2 pm	2 pm
3 pm	3 pm
4 pm	4 pm
5 pm	5 pm
6 pm	6 pm
Notes:	Notes:

Date:	Date:
6 am	6 am
7 am	7 am
8 am	8 am
9 am	9 am
10 am	10 am
11am	11am
12 noon	12 noon
1 pm	1 pm
2 pm	2 pm
3 pm	3 pm
4 pm	4 pm
5 pm	5 pm
6 pm	6 pm
Notes:	Notes:

Date:	Date:
6 am	6 am
7 am	7 am
8 am	8 am
9 am	9 am
10 am	10 am
11am	11am
12 noon	12 noon
1 pm	1 pm
2 pm	2 pm
3 pm	3 pm
4 pm	4 pm
5 pm	5 pm
6 pm	6 pm
Notes:	Notes:

Date:	Date:
6 am	6 am
7 am	7 am
8 am	8 am
9 am	9 am
10 am	10 am
11am	11am
12 noon	12 noon
1 pm	1 pm
2 pm	2 pm
3 pm	3 pm
4 pm	4 pm
5 pm	5 pm
6 pm	6 pm
Notes:	Notes:

Date:	Date:
6 am	6 am
7 am	7 am
8 am	8 am
9 am	9 am
10 am	10 am
11am	11am
12 noon	12 noon
1 pm	1 pm
2 pm	2 pm
3 pm	3 pm
4 pm	4 pm
5 pm	5 pm
6 pm	6 pm
Notes:	Notes:

Date:	Date:
6 am	6 am
7 am	7 am
8 am	8 am
9 am	9 am
10 am	10 am
11am	11am
12 noon	12 noon
1 pm	1 pm
2 pm	2 pm
3 pm	3 pm
4 pm	4 pm
5 pm	5 pm
6 pm	6 pm
Notes:	Notes:

Date:	Date:
6 am	6 am
7 am	7 am
8 am	8 am
9 am	9 am
10 am	10 am
11am	11am
12 noon	12 noon
1 pm	1 pm
2 pm	2 pm
3 pm	3 pm
4 pm	4 pm
5 pm	5 pm
6 pm	6 pm
Notes:	Notes:

Date:	Date:
6 am	6 am
7 am	7 am
8 am	8 am
9 am	9 am
10 am	10 am
11am	11am
12 noon	12 noon
1 pm	1 pm
2 pm	2 pm
3 pm	3 pm
4 pm	4 pm
5 pm	5 pm
6 pm	6 pm
Notes:	Notes:

Date:

| 6 am |
| |
| 7 am |
| |
| 8 am |
| |
| 9 am |
| |
| 10 am |
| |
| 11am |
| |
| 12 noon |
| |
| 1 pm |
| |
| 2 pm |
| |
| 3 pm |
| |
| 4 pm |
| |
| 5 pm |
| |
| 6 pm |
| |
| |
| Notes: |
| |
| |
| |
| |
| |
| |
| |

Date:

| 6 am |
| |
| 7 am |
| |
| 8 am |
| |
| 9 am |
| |
| 10 am |
| |
| 11am |
| |
| 12 noon |
| |
| 1 pm |
| |
| 2 pm |
| |
| 3 pm |
| |
| 4 pm |
| |
| 5 pm |
| |
| 6 pm |
| |
| |
| Notes: |
| |
| |
| |
| |
| |
| |
| |

Date:	Date:
6 am	6 am
7 am	7 am
8 am	8 am
9 am	9 am
10 am	10 am
11am	11am
12 noon	12 noon
1 pm	1 pm
2 pm	2 pm
3 pm	3 pm
4 pm	4 pm
5 pm	5 pm
6 pm	6 pm
Notes:	Notes:

Date:	Date:
6 am	6 am
7 am	7 am
8 am	8 am
9 am	9 am
10 am	10 am
11am	11am
12 noon	12 noon
1 pm	1 pm
2 pm	2 pm
3 pm	3 pm
4 pm	4 pm
5 pm	5 pm
6 pm	6 pm
Notes:	Notes:

Date:	Date:
6 am	6 am
7 am	7 am
8 am	8 am
9 am	9 am
10 am	10 am
11am	11am
12 noon	12 noon
1 pm	1 pm
2 pm	2 pm
3 pm	3 pm
4 pm	4 pm
5 pm	5 pm
6 pm	6 pm
Notes:	Notes:

Date:	Date:
6 am	6 am
7 am	7 am
8 am	8 am
9 am	9 am
10 am	10 am
11am	11am
12 noon	12 noon
1 pm	1 pm
2 pm	2 pm
3 pm	3 pm
4 pm	4 pm
5 pm	5 pm
6 pm	6 pm
Notes:	Notes:

Date:	Date:
6 am	6 am
7 am	7 am
8 am	8 am
9 am	9 am
10 am	10 am
11am	11am
12 noon	12 noon
1 pm	1 pm
2 pm	2 pm
3 pm	3 pm
4 pm	4 pm
5 pm	5 pm
6 pm	6 pm
Notes:	Notes:

Date:	Date:
6 am	6 am
7 am	7 am
8 am	8 am
9 am	9 am
10 am	10 am
11am	11am
12 noon	12 noon
1 pm	1 pm
2 pm	2 pm
3 pm	3 pm
4 pm	4 pm
5 pm	5 pm
6 pm	6 pm
Notes:	Notes:

Date: | Date:

6 am	6 am
7 am	7 am
8 am	8 am
9 am	9 am
10 am	10 am
11am	11am
12 noon	12 noon
1 pm	1 pm
2 pm	2 pm
3 pm	3 pm
4 pm	4 pm
5 pm	5 pm
6 pm	6 pm
Notes:	Notes:

Date:	Date:
6 am	6 am
7 am	7 am
8 am	8 am
9 am	9 am
10 am	10 am
11am	11am
12 noon	12 noon
1 pm	1 pm
2 pm	2 pm
3 pm	3 pm
4 pm	4 pm
5 pm	5 pm
6 pm	6 pm
Notes:	Notes:

Date:	Date:
6 am	6 am
7 am	7 am
8 am	8 am
9 am	9 am
10 am	10 am
11am	11am
12 noon	12 noon
1 pm	1 pm
2 pm	2 pm
3 pm	3 pm
4 pm	4 pm
5 pm	5 pm
6 pm	6 pm
Notes:	Notes:

Date:	Date:
6 am	6 am
7 am	7 am
8 am	8 am
9 am	9 am
10 am	10 am
11am	11am
12 noon	12 noon
1 pm	1 pm
2 pm	2 pm
3 pm	3 pm
4 pm	4 pm
5 pm	5 pm
6 pm	6 pm
Notes:	Notes:

Date:	Date:
6 am	6 am
7 am	7 am
8 am	8 am
9 am	9 am
10 am	10 am
11am	11am
12 noon	12 noon
1 pm	1 pm
2 pm	2 pm
3 pm	3 pm
4 pm	4 pm
5 pm	5 pm
6 pm	6 pm
Notes:	Notes:

Date:		Date:	
6 am		6 am	
7 am		7 am	
8 am		8 am	
9 am		9 am	
10 am		10 am	
11am		11am	
12 noon		12 noon	
1 pm		1 pm	
2 pm		2 pm	
3 pm		3 pm	
4 pm		4 pm	
5 pm		5 pm	
6 pm		6 pm	
Notes:		Notes:	

Date: _____ | Date: _____

6 am	6 am
7 am	7 am
8 am	8 am
9 am	9 am
10 am	10 am
11am	11am
12 noon	12 noon
1 pm	1 pm
2 pm	2 pm
3 pm	3 pm
4 pm	4 pm
5 pm	5 pm
6 pm	6 pm
Notes:	Notes:

Date:	Date:
6 am	6 am
7 am	7 am
8 am	8 am
9 am	9 am
10 am	10 am
11am	11am
12 noon	12 noon
1 pm	1 pm
2 pm	2 pm
3 pm	3 pm
4 pm	4 pm
5 pm	5 pm
6 pm	6 pm
Notes:	Notes:

Date:	Date:
6 am	6 am
7 am	7 am
8 am	8 am
9 am	9 am
10 am	10 am
11am	11am
12 noon	12 noon
1 pm	1 pm
2 pm	2 pm
3 pm	3 pm
4 pm	4 pm
5 pm	5 pm
6 pm	6 pm
Notes:	Notes:

Date:	Date:
6 am	6 am
7 am	7 am
8 am	8 am
9 am	9 am
10 am	10 am
11am	11am
12 noon	12 noon
1 pm	1 pm
2 pm	2 pm
3 pm	3 pm
4 pm	4 pm
5 pm	5 pm
6 pm	6 pm
Notes:	Notes:

Date:	Date:
6 am	6 am
7 am	7 am
8 am	8 am
9 am	9 am
10 am	10 am
11am	11am
12 noon	12 noon
1 pm	1 pm
2 pm	2 pm
3 pm	3 pm
4 pm	4 pm
5 pm	5 pm
6 pm	6 pm
Notes:	Notes:

Date:	Date:
6 am	6 am
7 am	7 am
8 am	8 am
9 am	9 am
10 am	10 am
11am	11am
12 noon	12 noon
1 pm	1 pm
2 pm	2 pm
3 pm	3 pm
4 pm	4 pm
5 pm	5 pm
6 pm	6 pm
Notes:	Notes:

Date:	Date:
6 am	6 am
7 am	7 am
8 am	8 am
9 am	9 am
10 am	10 am
11am	11am
12 noon	12 noon
1 pm	1 pm
2 pm	2 pm
3 pm	3 pm
4 pm	4 pm
5 pm	5 pm
6 pm	6 pm
Notes:	Notes:

Date:	Date:
6 am	6 am
7 am	7 am
8 am	8 am
9 am	9 am
10 am	10 am
11am	11am
12 noon	12 noon
1 pm	1 pm
2 pm	2 pm
3 pm	3 pm
4 pm	4 pm
5 pm	5 pm
6 pm	6 pm
Notes:	Notes:

Date:	Date:
6 am	6 am
7 am	7 am
8 am	8 am
9 am	9 am
10 am	10 am
11am	11am
12 noon	12 noon
1 pm	1 pm
2 pm	2 pm
3 pm	3 pm
4 pm	4 pm
5 pm	5 pm
6 pm	6 pm
Notes:	Notes:

Date:	Date:
6 am	6 am
7 am	7 am
8 am	8 am
9 am	9 am
10 am	10 am
11am	11am
12 noon	12 noon
1 pm	1 pm
2 pm	2 pm
3 pm	3 pm
4 pm	4 pm
5 pm	5 pm
6 pm	6 pm
Notes:	Notes:

Date:	Date:
6 am	6 am
7 am	7 am
8 am	8 am
9 am	9 am
10 am	10 am
11am	11am
12 noon	12 noon
1 pm	1 pm
2 pm	2 pm
3 pm	3 pm
4 pm	4 pm
5 pm	5 pm
6 pm	6 pm
Notes:	Notes:

Date:	Date:
6 am	6 am
7 am	7 am
8 am	8 am
9 am	9 am
10 am	10 am
11am	11am
12 noon	12 noon
1 pm	1 pm
2 pm	2 pm
3 pm	3 pm
4 pm	4 pm
5 pm	5 pm
6 pm	6 pm
Notes:	Notes:

Date:	Date:
6 am	6 am
7 am	7 am
8 am	8 am
9 am	9 am
10 am	10 am
11am	11am
12 noon	12 noon
1 pm	1 pm
2 pm	2 pm
3 pm	3 pm
4 pm	4 pm
5 pm	5 pm
6 pm	6 pm
Notes:	Notes:

Date:		Date:	
6 am		6 am	
7 am		7 am	
8 am		8 am	
9 am		9 am	
10 am		10 am	
11am		11am	
12 noon		12 noon	
1 pm		1 pm	
2 pm		2 pm	
3 pm		3 pm	
4 pm		4 pm	
5 pm		5 pm	
6 pm		6 pm	
Notes:		Notes:	

Date:	Date:
6 am	6 am
7 am	7 am
8 am	8 am
9 am	9 am
10 am	10 am
11am	11am
12 noon	12 noon
1 pm	1 pm
2 pm	2 pm
3 pm	3 pm
4 pm	4 pm
5 pm	5 pm
6 pm	6 pm
Notes:	Notes:

Date:	Date:
6 am	6 am
7 am	7 am
8 am	8 am
9 am	9 am
10 am	10 am
11am	11am
12 noon	12 noon
1 pm	1 pm
2 pm	2 pm
3 pm	3 pm
4 pm	4 pm
5 pm	5 pm
6 pm	6 pm
Notes:	Notes:

Date:		Date:	
6 am		6 am	
7 am		7 am	
8 am		8 am	
9 am		9 am	
10 am		10 am	
11am		11am	
12 noon		12 noon	
1 pm		1 pm	
2 pm		2 pm	
3 pm		3 pm	
4 pm		4 pm	
5 pm		5 pm	
6 pm		6 pm	
Notes:		Notes:	

Date:	Date:
6 am	6 am
7 am	7 am
8 am	8 am
9 am	9 am
10 am	10 am
11am	11am
12 noon	12 noon
1 pm	1 pm
2 pm	2 pm
3 pm	3 pm
4 pm	4 pm
5 pm	5 pm
6 pm	6 pm
Notes:	Notes:

Date:	Date:
6 am	6 am
7 am	7 am
8 am	8 am
9 am	9 am
10 am	10 am
11am	11am
12 noon	12 noon
1 pm	1 pm
2 pm	2 pm
3 pm	3 pm
4 pm	4 pm
5 pm	5 pm
6 pm	6 pm
Notes:	Notes:

Date:	Date:
6 am	6 am
7 am	7 am
8 am	8 am
9 am	9 am
10 am	10 am
11am	11am
12 noon	12 noon
1 pm	1 pm
2 pm	2 pm
3 pm	3 pm
4 pm	4 pm
5 pm	5 pm
6 pm	6 pm
Notes:	Notes:

Date:	Date:
6 am	6 am
7 am	7 am
8 am	8 am
9 am	9 am
10 am	10 am
11am	11am
12 noon	12 noon
1 pm	1 pm
2 pm	2 pm
3 pm	3 pm
4 pm	4 pm
5 pm	5 pm
6 pm	6 pm
Notes:	Notes:

Date: _____   Date: _____

6 am		6 am	
7 am		7 am	
8 am		8 am	
9 am		9 am	
10 am		10 am	
11am		11am	
12 noon		12 noon	
1 pm		1 pm	
2 pm		2 pm	
3 pm		3 pm	
4 pm		4 pm	
5 pm		5 pm	
6 pm		6 pm	
Notes:		Notes:	

Date:	Date:
6 am	6 am
7 am	7 am
8 am	8 am
9 am	9 am
10 am	10 am
11am	11am
12 noon	12 noon
1 pm	1 pm
2 pm	2 pm
3 pm	3 pm
4 pm	4 pm
5 pm	5 pm
6 pm	6 pm
Notes:	Notes:

Date:	Date:
6 am	6 am
7 am	7 am
8 am	8 am
9 am	9 am
10 am	10 am
11am	11am
12 noon	12 noon
1 pm	1 pm
2 pm	2 pm
3 pm	3 pm
4 pm	4 pm
5 pm	5 pm
6 pm	6 pm
Notes:	Notes:

Date:	Date:
6 am	6 am
7 am	7 am
8 am	8 am
9 am	9 am
10 am	10 am
11am	11am
12 noon	12 noon
1 pm	1 pm
2 pm	2 pm
3 pm	3 pm
4 pm	4 pm
5 pm	5 pm
6 pm	6 pm
Notes:	Notes:

Date:	Date:
6 am	6 am
7 am	7 am
8 am	8 am
9 am	9 am
10 am	10 am
11am	11am
12 noon	12 noon
1 pm	1 pm
2 pm	2 pm
3 pm	3 pm
4 pm	4 pm
5 pm	5 pm
6 pm	6 pm
Notes:	Notes:

Date:	Date:
6 am	6 am
7 am	7 am
8 am	8 am
9 am	9 am
10 am	10 am
11am	11am
12 noon	12 noon
1 pm	1 pm
2 pm	2 pm
3 pm	3 pm
4 pm	4 pm
5 pm	5 pm
6 pm	6 pm
Notes:	Notes:

Date:	Date:
6 am	6 am
7 am	7 am
8 am	8 am
9 am	9 am
10 am	10 am
11am	11am
12 noon	12 noon
1 pm	1 pm
2 pm	2 pm
3 pm	3 pm
4 pm	4 pm
5 pm	5 pm
6 pm	6 pm
Notes:	Notes:

Date:	Date:
6 am	6 am
7 am	7 am
8 am	8 am
9 am	9 am
10 am	10 am
11am	11am
12 noon	12 noon
1 pm	1 pm
2 pm	2 pm
3 pm	3 pm
4 pm	4 pm
5 pm	5 pm
6 pm	6 pm
Notes:	Notes:

Date:	Date:
6 am	6 am
7 am	7 am
8 am	8 am
9 am	9 am
10 am	10 am
11am	11am
12 noon	12 noon
1 pm	1 pm
2 pm	2 pm
3 pm	3 pm
4 pm	4 pm
5 pm	5 pm
6 pm	6 pm
Notes:	Notes:

Date:	Date:
6 am	6 am
7 am	7 am
8 am	8 am
9 am	9 am
10 am	10 am
11am	11am
12 noon	12 noon
1 pm	1 pm
2 pm	2 pm
3 pm	3 pm
4 pm	4 pm
5 pm	5 pm
6 pm	6 pm
Notes:	Notes:

Date:	Date:
6 am	6 am
7 am	7 am
8 am	8 am
9 am	9 am
10 am	10 am
11am	11am
12 noon	12 noon
1 pm	1 pm
2 pm	2 pm
3 pm	3 pm
4 pm	4 pm
5 pm	5 pm
6 pm	6 pm
Notes:	Notes:

Date:	Date:
6 am	6 am
7 am	7 am
8 am	8 am
9 am	9 am
10 am	10 am
11am	11am
12 noon	12 noon
1 pm	1 pm
2 pm	2 pm
3 pm	3 pm
4 pm	4 pm
5 pm	5 pm
6 pm	6 pm
Notes:	Notes:

Date:	Date:
6 am	6 am
7 am	7 am
8 am	8 am
9 am	9 am
10 am	10 am
11am	11am
12 noon	12 noon
1 pm	1 pm
2 pm	2 pm
3 pm	3 pm
4 pm	4 pm
5 pm	5 pm
6 pm	6 pm
Notes:	Notes:

Date:	Date:
6 am	6 am
7 am	7 am
8 am	8 am
9 am	9 am
10 am	10 am
11am	11am
12 noon	12 noon
1 pm	1 pm
2 pm	2 pm
3 pm	3 pm
4 pm	4 pm
5 pm	5 pm
6 pm	6 pm
Notes:	Notes:

Date:	Date:
6 am	6 am
7 am	7 am
8 am	8 am
9 am	9 am
10 am	10 am
11am	11am
12 noon	12 noon
1 pm	1 pm
2 pm	2 pm
3 pm	3 pm
4 pm	4 pm
5 pm	5 pm
6 pm	6 pm
Notes:	Notes:

Date:	Date:
6 am	6 am
7 am	7 am
8 am	8 am
9 am	9 am
10 am	10 am
11am	11am
12 noon	12 noon
1 pm	1 pm
2 pm	2 pm
3 pm	3 pm
4 pm	4 pm
5 pm	5 pm
6 pm	6 pm
Notes:	Notes:

Date: _____   Date: _____

6 am	6 am
7 am	7 am
8 am	8 am
9 am	9 am
10 am	10 am
11am	11am
12 noon	12 noon
1 pm	1 pm
2 pm	2 pm
3 pm	3 pm
4 pm	4 pm
5 pm	5 pm
6 pm	6 pm
Notes:	Notes:

Date:	Date:
6 am	6 am
7 am	7 am
8 am	8 am
9 am	9 am
10 am	10 am
11am	11am
12 noon	12 noon
1 pm	1 pm
2 pm	2 pm
3 pm	3 pm
4 pm	4 pm
5 pm	5 pm
6 pm	6 pm
Notes:	Notes:

Date:	Date:
6 am	6 am
7 am	7 am
8 am	8 am
9 am	9 am
10 am	10 am
11am	11am
12 noon	12 noon
1 pm	1 pm
2 pm	2 pm
3 pm	3 pm
4 pm	4 pm
5 pm	5 pm
6 pm	6 pm
Notes:	Notes:

Date: Date:

6 am	6 am
7 am	7 am
8 am	8 am
9 am	9 am
10 am	10 am
11am	11am
12 noon	12 noon
1 pm	1 pm
2 pm	2 pm
3 pm	3 pm
4 pm	4 pm
5 pm	5 pm
6 pm	6 pm
Notes:	Notes:

Date: | Date:

6 am	6 am
7 am	7 am
8 am	8 am
9 am	9 am
10 am	10 am
11am	11am
12 noon	12 noon
1 pm	1 pm
2 pm	2 pm
3 pm	3 pm
4 pm	4 pm
5 pm	5 pm
6 pm	6 pm
Notes:	Notes:

Date:	Date:
6 am	6 am
7 am	7 am
8 am	8 am
9 am	9 am
10 am	10 am
11am	11am
12 noon	12 noon
1 pm	1 pm
2 pm	2 pm
3 pm	3 pm
4 pm	4 pm
5 pm	5 pm
6 pm	6 pm
Notes:	Notes:

Date: _____

6 am
7 am
8 am
9 am
10 am
11am
12 noon
1 pm
2 pm
3 pm
4 pm
5 pm
6 pm
Notes:

Date: _____

6 am
7 am
8 am
9 am
10 am
11am
12 noon
1 pm
2 pm
3 pm
4 pm
5 pm
6 pm
Notes:

Date:	Date:
6 am	6 am
7 am	7 am
8 am	8 am
9 am	9 am
10 am	10 am
11am	11am
12 noon	12 noon
1 pm	1 pm
2 pm	2 pm
3 pm	3 pm
4 pm	4 pm
5 pm	5 pm
6 pm	6 pm
Notes:	Notes:

Date:	Date:
6 am	6 am
7 am	7 am
8 am	8 am
9 am	9 am
10 am	10 am
11am	11am
12 noon	12 noon
1 pm	1 pm
2 pm	2 pm
3 pm	3 pm
4 pm	4 pm
5 pm	5 pm
6 pm	6 pm
Notes:	Notes:

Date:	Date:
6 am	6 am
7 am	7 am
8 am	8 am
9 am	9 am
10 am	10 am
11am	11am
12 noon	12 noon
1 pm	1 pm
2 pm	2 pm
3 pm	3 pm
4 pm	4 pm
5 pm	5 pm
6 pm	6 pm
Notes:	Notes:

Date: | Date:

6 am	6 am
7 am	7 am
8 am	8 am
9 am	9 am
10 am	10 am
11am	11am
12 noon	12 noon
1 pm	1 pm
2 pm	2 pm
3 pm	3 pm
4 pm	4 pm
5 pm	5 pm
6 pm	6 pm
Notes:	Notes:

Date:	Date:
6 am	6 am
7 am	7 am
8 am	8 am
9 am	9 am
10 am	10 am
11am	11am
12 noon	12 noon
1 pm	1 pm
2 pm	2 pm
3 pm	3 pm
4 pm	4 pm
5 pm	5 pm
6 pm	6 pm
Notes:	Notes:

Date:	Date:
6 am	6 am
7 am	7 am
8 am	8 am
9 am	9 am
10 am	10 am
11am	11am
12 noon	12 noon
1 pm	1 pm
2 pm	2 pm
3 pm	3 pm
4 pm	4 pm
5 pm	5 pm
6 pm	6 pm
Notes:	Notes:

2014

January
S	M	T	W	T	F	S
			1	2	3	4
5	6	7	8	9	10	11
12	13	14	15	16	17	18
19	20	21	22	23	24	25
26	27	28	29	30	31	

February
S	M	T	W	T	F	S
						1
2	3	4	5	6	7	8
9	10	11	12	13	14	15
16	17	18	19	20	21	22
23	24	25	26	27	28	

March
S	M	T	W	T	F	S
						1
2	3	4	5	6	7	8
9	10	11	12	13	14	15
16	17	18	19	20	21	22
23	24	25	26	27	28	29
30	31					

April
S	M	T	W	T	F	S
		1	2	3	4	5
6	7	8	9	10	11	12
13	14	15	16	17	18	19
20	21	22	23	24	25	26
27	28	29	30			

May
S	M	T	W	T	F	S
				1	2	3
4	5	6	7	8	9	10
11	12	13	14	15	16	17
18	19	20	21	22	23	24
25	26	27	28	29	30	31

June
S	M	T	W	T	F	S
1	2	3	4	5	6	7
8	9	10	11	12	13	14
15	16	17	18	19	20	21
22	23	24	25	26	27	28
29	30					

July
S	M	T	W	T	F	S
		1	2	3	4	5
6	7	8	9	10	11	12
13	14	15	16	17	18	19
20	21	22	23	24	25	26
27	28	29	30	31		

August
S	M	T	W	T	F	S
					1	2
3	4	5	6	7	8	9
10	11	12	13	14	15	16
17	18	19	20	21	22	23
24	25	26	27	28	29	30
31						

September
S	M	T	W	T	F	S
	1	2	3	4	5	6
7	8	9	10	11	12	13
14	15	16	17	18	19	20
21	22	23	24	25	26	27
28	29	30				

October
S	M	T	W	T	F	S
			1	2	3	4
5	6	7	8	9	10	11
12	13	14	15	16	17	18
19	20	21	22	23	24	25
26	27	28	29	30	31	

November
S	M	T	W	T	F	S
						1
2	3	4	5	6	7	8
9	10	11	12	13	14	15
16	17	18	19	20	21	22
23	24	25	26	27	28	29
30						

December
S	M	T	W	T	F	S
	1	2	3	4	5	6
7	8	9	10	11	12	13
14	15	16	17	18	19	20
21	22	23	24	25	26	27
28	29	30	31			

2015

January
S	M	T	W	T	F	S
				1	2	3
4	5	6	7	8	9	10
11	12	13	14	15	16	17
18	19	20	21	22	23	24
25	26	27	28	29	30	31

February
S	M	T	W	T	F	S
1	2	3	4	5	6	7
8	9	10	11	12	13	14
15	16	17	18	19	20	21
22	23	24	25	26	27	28

March
S	M	T	W	T	F	S
1	2	3	4	5	6	7
8	9	10	11	12	13	14
15	16	17	18	19	20	21
22	23	24	25	26	27	28
29	30	31				

April
S	M	T	W	T	F	S
			1	2	3	4
5	6	7	8	9	10	11
12	13	14	15	16	17	18
19	20	21	22	23	24	25
26	27	28	29	30		

May
S	M	T	W	T	F	S
					1	2
3	4	5	6	7	8	9
10	11	12	13	14	15	16
17	18	19	20	21	22	23
24	25	26	27	28	29	30
31						

June
S	M	T	W	T	F	S
	1	2	3	4	5	6
7	8	9	10	11	12	13
14	15	16	17	18	19	20
21	22	23	24	25	26	27
28	29	30				

July
S	M	T	W	T	F	S
			1	2	3	4
5	6	7	8	9	10	11
12	13	14	15	16	17	18
19	20	21	22	23	24	25
26	27	28	29	30	31	

August
S	M	T	W	T	F	S
						1
2	3	4	5	6	7	8
9	10	11	12	13	14	15
16	17	18	19	20	21	22
23	24	25	26	27	28	29
30	31					

September
S	M	T	W	T	F	S
		1	2	3	4	5
6	7	8	9	10	11	12
13	14	15	16	17	18	19
20	21	22	23	24	25	26
27	28	29	30			

October
S	M	T	W	T	F	S
				1	2	3
4	5	6	7	8	9	10
11	12	13	14	15	16	17
18	19	20	21	22	23	24
25	26	27	28	29	30	31

November
S	M	T	W	T	F	S
1	2	3	4	5	6	7
8	9	10	11	12	13	14
15	16	17	18	19	20	21
22	23	24	25	26	27	28
29	30					

December
S	M	T	W	T	F	S
		1	2	3	4	5
6	7	8	9	10	11	12
13	14	15	16	17	18	19
20	21	22	23	24	25	26
27	28	29	30	31		